A BRAND
IN YOUR HAND

A BRAND IN YOUR HAND

A Simple Guide to Defining YOU or YOUR Business to the World

Created and
Written by
Glenn Rudin

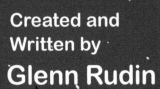

Illustrated by
Niki Giokas

Always Been Creative Press
www.alwaysbeencreative.com

Ordering Information:
Quantity sales. Special discounts are available on quantity purchases by corporations, associations, for fundraising or educational needs. For details, contact glenn@ alwaysbeencreative.com.

Book design: Christy Collins, Constellation Book Services
Illustrator: Niki Giokas
Publishing consultant: Martha Bullen, Bullen Publishing Services

ISBN (paperback): 978-1-7369964-0-9
ISBN (ebook): 978-1-7369964-1-6

Printed in the United States of America

A BRAND IN YOUR HAND is dedicated to:

The dreamers, the entrepreneurs,
those pivoting to new horizons
and the students around the world who
are just beginning their personal journey.

I hope my book enlightens you, energizes you
and ultimately shortens your passage
from where you are to the great places you are headed.

If even one person's journey is shortened or made
more pleasant, then **A BRAND IN YOUR HAND**
will have met one of its key goals.

I know you can do this, I believe in your dream
In no time at all you'll be floating downstream...

It's nice to meet you....

Do you have a new venture that you'd like to pursue?
A new business idea burning inside of you?
If this is something you've been thinking about
You've come to the right place to sort it all out.

To get your new business launched off the ground
I have some guidance you'll find is quite sound.
In the business world, I'm an entrepreneur.
When it comes to branding I've got answers galore.

My advice comes from experience I've gained on my way.
My career started years ago and runs right through today.
It took me many years to build this knowledge base
Now, if you'll permit me, I'll begin to state my case.

A key part of your business will be your brand
It's something important you must understand.
On the following pages I will provide
A clear, comprehensive brand-building guide.

A brand name is a way to make a business stand out
It makes it more noticeable and gives it more clout.
When your branding's on point, it adds to its mystique.
This makes us feel like it's special and unique

Your brand will remind us of what you're about
It creates a strong message and leaves little doubt.
It's what we'll think about you, when you're not around
When done really well it should be quite profound.

In business and life we judge things super fast
And a brand that's not strong will simply not last.
The verses in my book will provide some direction
For your brand to look good when it's under inspection.

Of course it is possible, this could be really big
Your brand could provide you with an incredible gig.
So don't keep it cooped up inside of your head
Start working on making it happen instead.

So grab a sharp pencil now as you begin
I've included some charts I hope you'll fill in.
As you complete each section I hope you will see
How much fun building your own brand can be.

But nothing can happen until you have started.
Now is the time to get your course charted.
You have a lot to offer, so let's agree
You have got a brand that the world needs to see!

Audience

—Just Who Wants What You're Selling?

First, you've got to know who your audience is.
Because they are the reason to start any biz.
Which market segment will your brand address?
Who are the customers you'd like to impress?

Is your brand for women or strictly for men?
Or is it for those who want to marry again?
Now this is important, just who will you woo?
Which customers are likely to buy something from you?

Research your clients so you know who they are.
Do they live on your block or come from afar?
Where are they going, and where might they have been?
And will your idea be the yang for their yin?

Seek out your library, they've got data galore.
Then head to the internet where you'll find even more.
Create a profile of the people you're seeking
This is a process that requires lots of tweaking.

Are they younger or older or somewhere in between?
Are they avid consumers or prefer to live green?
Do they buy lots of toys for the kids in their house?
Or are they customers who buy gifts for their spouse?

Are they tall or short? Do they buy lots of shoes?
Do they like rock and roll? Or get down with the blues?
Give them a once over, know them through and through
Then try to see the world from their point of view.

Now that you've analyzed them up and down
And you know what makes them smile or frown
You'll start to develop your brand's appeal
And how it should make your audience feel.

Make sure you know your audience inside and out
And all of your research seems to check out.
Your momentum is building, your wheels are turning.
There's no stopping you now — read on and keep learning.

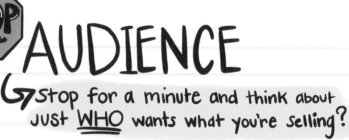

AUDIENCE

Stop for a minute and think about just **WHO** wants what you're selling?

Target Gender:

Location:

Age Range:

Income Level:

Education?:

Family Status:

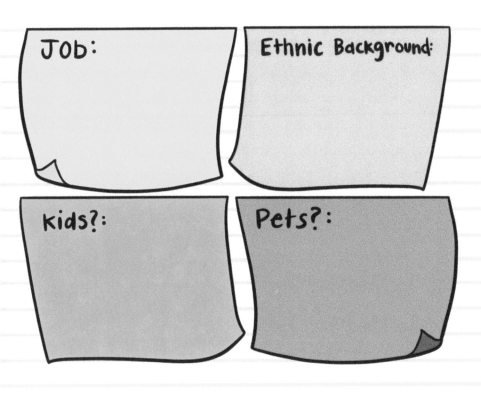

Job:

Ethnic Background:

Kids?:

Pets?:

→ Keys for this group: Charitable? Healthy? Green? Religious?

→ How does my brand fit into this group? Why is it important to them?

You can download this chart at:
www.ABrandInYourHand.com

MISSION STATEMENT
—Just Why Are You Doing This?—

Before you can earn your audience's trust
Defining your mission is a definite must.
Just what are the problems that your brand will solve?
Will what you're proposing cause us to evolve?

What is the value your brand will be bringing?
What praises do you want your customers singing?
What is the first thing that comes to their mind?
How will you leave your competition behind?

You need to feel strongly that this is your "Why."
You feel it so deeply it could make you cry.
This is passion you want them to feel
To pursue your brand because it's for real.

This is the summit you aspire to reach
The topic about which you're inspired to preach.
When you appeal to them in this meaningful way
You develop fans who are not likely to stray.

Now seeing your calling in black and in white
Brings the clarity you need to begin to take flight.
Record your brand's mission and commit yourself to it
Believe in your journey and make sure you pursue it.

STOP Your Mission Statement

↳ Stop for a minute and think about what your mission statement is...

Create a Mission Statement based on your and your company's passions:

→

What are you
Passionate
about and
Why?

→

What is
your Company
Passionate about
and Why?

→

What are some
"key words"
that describe
this passion?

→
→
→

YOUR PERSONAL BRAND
~you are the Star!

So, just what exactly is your "Personal Brand"?
It's the impression we get as we shake your hand.
What's the first thing that will come to our mind?
You'll want us to think we've made quite a find.

You need to define ways in which we perceive you.
You must be authentic if we're to believe you.
When your personal brand is misunderstood
Your message is confusing, and that isn't good.

This is important, so consider my advice
If your branding's too radical you might pay a price.
Its appearance should never detract from your vision
Or cause your audience to make an unwanted decision.

When you deliver your message to people you meet
You'll want to make sure that your story's complete.
With details that will tell them that you can be trusted
And you know your facts and are quite well adjusted.

For your personal brand, you are the star!
Your brand is carried wherever you are.
What you stand for is conveyed by you being you
In the things that you say and the things that you do.

That doesn't mean your brand can't be changed
And the way that we see you could be rearranged.
But this talk of a change is a bit premature.
Let's start with a look deep inside your core.

Consider your life and the things you've been through.
Your ideas and beliefs didn't come out of the blue.
The thoughts that you have were formed on your way.
They are based on your life up to today.

This all really started when you were a kid.
You watched the adults and you saw what they did.
Sometimes their actions would make you feel swell
But other times those actions did not go down well.

Then there was college and meeting new friends
Where you were exposed to a lot of new trends.
You learned many new things and as a result
You started to think differently as an adult.

All these experiences formed the tapestry of you
And you communicate this by the things that you do.
The opinions you have and the words that you say
The things you find meaningful and focus on each day.

Personal and business brands should be in sync
When they're not aligned we don't know what to think.
Your appearance should relate to your company's theme
We should get the idea you are on the same team.

25

So when you go out, it's best to prepare
Since we notice your clothes and the style of your hair.
Before you even have the chance to say "Hi"
You might turn us off, and we won't tell you why.

These rules all apply to the digital world.
The virtual space where your brand gets unfurled.
We can still see you when we're not face to face
Be professional whenever you appear in this space.

Be creative and original but with boundaries in mind
Don't scare off customers before your deal's signed.
Once we get to know just how talented you are
We'll have confidence your ideas can really go far.

You must be aware of your personal brand
And try your best to always be in command.
So be clear and committed to just who you are
And consistent when displaying your repertoire.

My Personal Brand

↳ Stop for a minute and think about who YOU are...

Where am I from?:

Am I quiet or loud?:

Energetic or reserved?:

My dress code is:

My education:

My parents were:

Circle ③ words that relate to you:

modern   techy

     reserved   relaxed

Smart   loud

     creative   Soft-spoken

Conservative   experienced

     energetic   aggressive

funny   confident

→ Words that best describe me? Ex: Shy, old-fashioned, outgoing, modern, hip, bold...

→ Want people to percieve me as? Ex: Funny, professional, serious, expert, outspoken...

→ Changes I want to make to my brand:

You can download this chart at:
www.ABrandInYourHand.com

Nonverbal branding is done without a word.
When it is not in balance you may look absurd.
Your posture, your clothes and, of course, how you speak
Should make you a person we will want to seek.

You can experiment with your nonverbal branding
But do not go so far as to impact your standing.
This is why knowing your audience is key.
How much will they accept before they turn and flee?

When you are addressing a person or a crowd
You must make eye contact to show you are proud.
Little gestures like this even if you aren't speaking
Can always be improved with a small amount of tweaking.

People can be shallow and you will discover
It is true that we do judge a book by its cover.
In just a few seconds we've made up our mind
Before you start speaking you have been defined.

Consider all this before you utter word one
Organize yourself so your job can be done.
Your nonverbal messaging will mean quite a bit.
When we come in contact will we think you've got grit?

Your unspoken brand includes how you dress.
It's not becoming if you are a mess.
Your wardrobe is your wrapping, like the label on a jar.
When that label's not understood you may not go far.

Your posture is something that creates an impression.
The "it factor" is a concept that becomes our obsession.
But when you feel good about the mission you're on
You'll leave us no choice, we will want to hang on.

Then there's your attitude, which goes a long way
And silently tells us that you're here to stay.
When you and your brand give off a good vibe
There's a really good chance we'll want to subscribe.

So branding that is done in a nonverbal way
Can be as important as the things that you say.
You will tell us a lot without having to speak
 And we'll get the idea with our very first peek.

COMPETITION
WHO ELSE DOES WHAT YOU DO?

For the business you're in, where do competitors mingle?
You must understand this before you hang out your shingle.
What features and benefits do they seem to mention?
Take notice of the ways that they grab attention.

Your business needs ideas that make it unique
And benefits that customers will want to seek.
Differentiation separates you from the pack
And it is this distinction that will make us come back.

Are your products better, smarter, or easier to use?
Or can you develop an offer we just can't refuse?
Will working with you make our troubles disappear?
Or if we need to talk will you lend us an ear?

Research is important because you will find
Other people are in the business you had in mind.
Cultivate the traits that set your business apart
And stories that will capture your customer's heart.

This is the discovery that you will need to make
Find a new ingredient and bake it in your cake.
See a new angle and give us the clue
For this is the way your brand will break through.

YOUR BUSINESS BRAND

HOW DOES YOUR BRAND MAKE US FEEL?

How will your brand leave people feeling?
What about it makes it appealing?
Is it light-hearted, friendly, or laugh out loud funny?
Or serious about things like why we save money?

A great deal of your branding will be nonverbal too
Your marketing materials are speaking for you.
Websites, emails, handouts, ads and the rest
Must look like part of the very same quest.

So what will your brand make us want to discuss?
What's our motivation to hop on your bus?
Does your story have universal appeal?
Will we believe your brand is authentic and real?

What about your brand will make us explore
And once we research it, will we Google for more?
Make sure what you're selling is in good supply.
And be ready to ship it when we're ready to buy.

Your Business Brand

STOP for a minute and think about how your brand/company is unique in its market...

Imagine your business's location

MY BUSINESS NAME:

LOGO SKETCH:

BRAND COLORS

1.

2.

3.

Fill in your info:

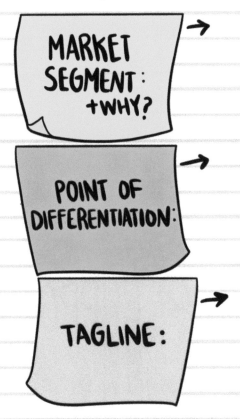

MARKET SEGMENT: +WHY? →

POINT OF DIFFERENTIATION: →

TAGLINE: →

List 3 key competitors, their websites, and what their specialty is (versus yours)...

1.

2.

3.

Features and benefits that make your brand unique
Must now be chosen for our attention to pique.
These features create the value of your brand
Make sure they are catchy instead of just bland.

Are you a Disney that's clean, wholesome and fun?
Or a Nike that motivates us to "Just Do It" and run?
You could be like Geico and save us some money
Or Progressive with Flo that just tries to be funny.

Do you sell insurance that protects us from trouble?
Or finance advice about a stock market bubble?
Maybe some type of service that makes our life easy?
Or high-tech advice to protect us from the sleazy?

What are the core values that define what you do?
What story will you tell so those traits will come through?
It's your story we'll remember long after it's told
That memory of your brand becomes marketing gold.

Features & Benefits

↳ stop for a minute and think about what the features and benefits of working with your brand/business are:

Feature - Something that your company, service or product has or is.
→ i.e. Subaru cars are very safe.

Think of up to 3 features of your brand:

Feature Example:
→ Better Quality!

Feature #1:

Feature #2:

Feature #3:

Benefit – The outcome or result that users will experience by using your company, service or product.

→ (i.e.) Subaru customers are less likely to be injured in an auto accident when in a Subaru.

Think of up to 3 benefits of your brand:

Benefit Example:
→ **Lasts Longer** :)

Benefit #1:

Benefit #2:

Benefit #3:

You can download this chart at: www.ABrandInYourHand.com

Your taglines and logos must be designed
So each time we see them your brand comes to mind.
A tagline that defines what your brand's all about
Summarizes your message and eliminates doubt.

Your logo should bring your business to life
So make it attractive and sharp as a knife.
Use colors and shapes that command our attention.
A distinctive font adds another dimension.

Do not be afraid to get help from some pros
An artist can design a logo that glows.
Writers can provide advice on your copy
They will make sure that your words aren't choppy.

Your Colors

Colors are important to highlight your brand.
They tell us a lot about what you have planned.
Brighter and bolder mean you want to stand out,
More muted choices say you don't want to shout.

Colors are a part of your nonverbal cues
Be very careful about which ones you choose.
Your colors will enhance your message and more
They'll provide texture for what you have in store.

These colors will be part of your entire brand suite
And all of your materials will look really neat.
Your website, brochures and the things that you print
Should all have a similar color scheme tint.

ELEVATOR PITCH

YOU'VE GOT 30 SECONDS TO IMPRESS US!

Your elevator pitch is the next thing to master
If you're unprepared it can be a disaster.
You've got just a few seconds to make an impression
To let us know why this is now your obsession.

For your elevator pitch I must persist
In just half a minute please give us the gist.
Of what you are offering and why it's so good
When you say it succinctly it will be understood.

Timing is crucial when presenting your pitch.
Prepare in advance to perform without a hitch.
30 seconds is your goal, no more and no less
If it's too long or too short, it could be a mess.

You perform your pitch as if you're on stage
There is an audience you must learn to engage.
Writing a script in advance is a must.
Practice your lines and you'll gain their trust.

Stand up and project the most confident you
The points you are making will come shining through.
Do this with passion and show that you care
Make eye contact — but you don't have to stare.

Self-belief is important, as is a good voice
Get your audience to listen, give them no choice.
To hear what you're saying and get just enough
To want more details about all of your stuff.

Consider the tone you'll want people to hear
The note that you're using will make your pitch clear.
Are you serious, fun, or passionate at heart?
Do you want to sound friendly or sound super smart?

Elevator pitches are not one size fits all
Think about who will be on your next call.
Customize the pitch so that each time you plead
You address each special audience's need.

Finally, practice until you have this down cold
Because when you are prepared it never gets old.
So be sure to rehearse the lines that you've chosen
Then you will perform them without getting frozen.

Messaging
What Should We Be Thinking?

Messaging is everything you say about your brand.
It's communications you make so we understand
Just why your brand is important to us
With lots of good info we'll want to discuss.

Make sure that your message is quite crystal clear
Keep it organized and concise and easy to hear.
You should be consistent with all that you say
As this is what keeps us from wandering away.

When we get your message, what thoughts come to mind?
Please don't make it something we'll have to unwind.
Stay with your plans and keep true to your story
Consistent communication is most mandatory.

Now that you have a new message to share
Don't be afraid to make buyers aware.
They need to know that you've got something new
And why, more than ever, they need it from you.

So...
What Did We Cover?

It's super important to consider your brand
To evaluate yourself and to know where you stand.
It's much deeper than just some product to sell
This is something on which you really should dwell.

When you move through the world, you'll leave an impression
And now armed with my verses you'll do this with discretion.
Pre-judging will happen wherever you go
But now you're aware and you'll be in the know.

Understand how your business is connected to you
Keep messages consistent so they come shining through.
Use the charts I've provided to establish your base
Take your time to think through this, it isn't a race.

Believe in your concept with all of your heart
You know you can do this, you know that you're smart.
Follow my steps and stick with me as a guide.
The time has come to take your brand for a ride.

You'll have our minds racing to hear what you've got.
There's lots of potential, you've got a great shot.
It's daring and clever and has value for us all
Your phone will be ringing, so answer our call.

Developing a brand is a journey for sure
And now you can build a foundational core.
Your plan is in motion, you've got wind in your sail
Just have faith in yourself as you blaze your new trail.

I hope you've enjoyed all my branding advice.
I've tried to be thorough while being concise.
After reading this book, I'm hoping you see
How important your brand's success is to me.

I would love to hear how you're doing so far
In your quest to become the next brand superstar.
Drop me a line — here's my contact address*
And fill me in on your newfound success.

*glenn@abrandinyourhand.com

Thanks for reading **A Brand In Your Hand**
I hope that my verses made you a fan.
If you know anyone with their own branding dream
Telling them about my book would be supreme.

One last thing while I have your attention
There's something else I wanted to mention.
If you've found that this book is ringing your bell
I've got more books coming that will teach you as well.

Glossary of Key Terms

1) **Audience**: Your audience is your targeted pool of potential customers based on the parameters you choose. You will want to narrow your audience down by using demographics to reduce the size of your potential customer base. When you narrow your audience to a particular niche (segment), it is far easier to create communications that are aimed specifically at them.

> Example: The primary audiences for A Brand in Your Hand are college-aged young adults and recent college graduates who are entering the work force. This audience has the most to gain by understanding the principles of this book. This book is also beneficial to young professionals and business owners who want to learn more about branding and marketing.

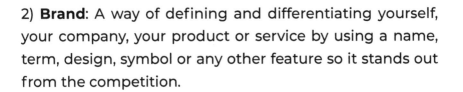

2) **Brand**: A way of defining and differentiating yourself, your company, your product or service by using a name, term, design, symbol or any other feature so it stands out from the competition.

> Example: Manufacturers of running and exercise shoes such as Nike, Adidas, New Balance, etc. use their brand names to further identify and differentiate their sneaker products from each other to consumers.

3) **Brand Messaging**: The values and ideas you or your company communicate verbally and nonverbally in all of your messaging and content about your products, services and the company itself.

Example: The Red Cross charity's brand message is all about help, relief and compassion. Any time you see any messaging from The Red Cross (which includes the well-known red cross symbol) you know the message relates to aiding victims of disasters and how consumers can help with their donations.

4) **Corporate Brand**: The ways a company differentiates itself, its products, employees or services from its competitors by using names, terms, designs, symbols, uniforms, colors, language, slogans or other features in the marketplace it operates in.

Example: Apple, the computer company, differentiates itself via branding with its Apple logo, sleek packaging, minimalist colors, store and product design, employee attire and the vibe it consistently gives off in every communication it makes to the world.

5) **Demographics**: Statistical data and information related to the population and particular groups within it.

Example: The entire population of the United States is roughly 330 million people. If you are marketing a

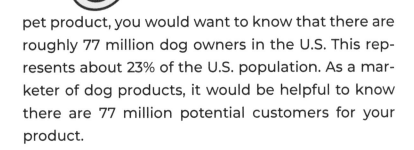

pet product, you would want to know that there are roughly 77 million dog owners in the U.S. This represents about 23% of the U.S. population. As a marketer of dog products, it would be helpful to know there are 77 million potential customers for your product.

6) **Differentiation**: A business strategy or plan to provide a product or service for customers that is different from the products or services that your competitors are offering. This is your competitive advantage, and it should constantly be highlighted in your communications to customers and potential customers. It is what makes your business, product or service unique.

> Example: In the fast food burger marketplace, Burger King's differentiation feature is their burger's "flame-broiled" taste. This taste feature differentiates Burger King from its key competitors, McDonald's and Wendy's, who do not offer flame-broiled burgers.

7) **Elevator Pitch**: A brief verbal or written summary that describes why you, your company, product or service is of interest to potential customers. This short speech should take about 30 seconds to verbalize and should create a high level of interest so that listeners want to hear more details.

8) **Logo**: The visual image we can see and identify as the trademark of your brand through the use of colors, elements and words that come together in a thumbnail of your brand.

> Example: The unmistakable golden arches which indicate a McDonald's hamburger outlet, ad, packaging, uniform, etc.

9) **Market Segment**: A part of a marketing strategy. In this strategy certain groups of consumers are selected so that the company's products can be presented in ways that appeal specifically to their interests.

> Example: Iams Pet food has identified a market segment of customers who believe in healthy food options for themselves, and are likely to want healthy options for their pets.

10) **Mission Statement**: A written description that details why your company was founded and why it exists. What is the purpose of your organization? What does it hope to accomplish as a result of what it is doing? This statement is the very heart of your organization, and when potential customers read it (and understand it) they should be inspired to patronize your products and services. A mission statement brings the focus of your company to life.

Example: Tesla's mission: To accelerate the world's transition to sustainable energy.

11) **Nonverbal Branding**: The various ways you can create an impression about your company, product, service or self without a spoken word. Anything that creates, changes or modifies an impression without using words is a nonverbal branding message.

Examples: Your clothing choices (business professional), your posture (standing up straight when you address people), your facial expression (smiling and kind) are some examples of how you can influence potential customers about yourself without even speaking. Your company can create its nonverbal branding with the use of colors and design in its logo and the images it uses in its advertisements and on its website.

12) **Personal Brand**: The impression, feeling or attitude that you convey to people when they come in contact with you, observe you, listen to you or interact with you in any way. Personal branding impressions are made within seconds of your being observed.

Example: Mary Richardson carefully managed her personal brand. She always dressed professionally and wore business suits when she knew she'd be

interacting with other corporate professionals or colleagues in a business setting. She was very careful not to mix her personal life with her professional life. There was never any confusion when it came to Mary's image. Her personal brand was always business professional.

13) Tagline: This is usually one line that summarizes what your brand's identity, purpose and values are all about. When done well the tagline will stick with your audience.

Examples:
Nationwide Insurance
Tagline: Nationwide is on your side.

Nike
Tagline: Just do it.

I would love to hear about your new brand
Did I provide you with a helping hand?
By now you've become a branding phenom
Let me know at ABrandInYourHand.com

Glenn@ABrandInYourHand.com

www.ABrandInYourHand.com

A BRAND IN YOUR HAND

* * * * * * * * * * * * * * * * * *

Use this journal to take notes, record your thoughts and develop important details.

Today is: /   /   I am working on my:

| **Non-Verbal Brand** | **Message** | **Colors** | **Elevator Pitch** | **Features** |
| **Personal Brand** | **Audience** | **Logo** | **Mission Statement** | **Benefits** |

_____

_____

_____

_____

_____

_____

_____

_____

_____

_____

_____

_____

_____

_____

_____

_____

_____

_____

_____

_____

_____

_____

_____

_____

_____

_____

_____

_____

_____

_____

"Nothing can happen until you have started...Now is the time to get your course charted..." Glenn Rudin

A BRAND IN YOUR HAND

Use this journal to take notes, record your thoughts and develop important details.

Today is: / / I am working on my:

| Non-Verbal Brand | Message | Colors | Elevator Pitch | Features |
| Personal Brand | Audience | Logo | Mission Statement | Benefits |

_____
_____
_____
_____
_____
_____
_____
_____
_____
_____
_____
_____
_____
_____
_____
_____
_____
_____
_____
_____
_____
_____
_____
_____
_____
_____
_____

"Nothing can happen until you have started...Now is the time to get your course charted..." Glenn Rudin

A BRAND IN YOUR HAND

Use this journal to take notes, record your thoughts and develop important details.

Today is: / / I am working on my:

| Non-Verbal Brand | Message | Colors | Elevator Pitch | Features |
| Personal Brand | Audience | Logo | Mission Statement | Benefits |

_____
_____
_____
_____
_____
_____
_____
_____
_____
_____
_____
_____
_____
_____
_____
_____
_____
_____
_____
_____
_____
_____
_____
_____
_____
_____
_____
_____

"Nothing can happen until you have started...Now is the time to get your course charted..." Glenn Rudin

* * * * * * * * * * * * * * * * * * *

A BRAND IN YOUR HAND

Use this journal to take notes, record your thoughts and develop important details.

Today is: / / I am working on my:

| Non-Verbal Brand | Message | Colors | Elevator Pitch | Features |
| Personal Brand | Audience | Logo | Mission Statement | Benefits |

_____
_____
_____
_____
_____
_____
_____
_____
_____
_____
_____
_____
_____
_____
_____
_____
_____
_____
_____
_____
_____
_____
_____
_____
_____
_____
_____

"Nothing can happen until you have started...Now is the time to get your course charted..." Glenn Rudin

★ ★ ★ ★ ★ ★ ★ ★ ★ ★ ★ ★ ★ ★ ★ ★ ★ ★

A BRAND IN YOUR HAND

Use this journal to take notes, record your thoughts and develop important details.

Today is: / / *I am working on my:*

| Non-Verbal Brand | Message | Colors | Elevator Pitch | Features |
| Personal Brand | Audience | Logo | Mission Statement | Benefits |

_____
_____
_____
_____
_____
_____
_____
_____
_____
_____
_____
_____
_____
_____
_____
_____
_____
_____
_____
_____
_____
_____
_____
_____
_____
_____
_____
_____
_____

"Nothing can happen until you have started...Now is the time to get your course charted..." Glenn Rudin

✴ ✴ ✴ ✴ ✴ ✴ ✴ ✴ ✴ ✴ ✴ ✴ ✴ ✴ ✴ ✴ ✴ ✴

A BRAND IN YOUR HAND

Use this journal to take notes, record your thoughts and develop important details.

Today is: / / I am working on my:

| Non-Verbal Brand | Message | Colors | Elevator Pitch | Features |
| Personal Brand | Audience | Logo | Mission Statement | Benefits |

_____
_____
_____
_____
_____
_____
_____
_____
_____
_____
_____
_____
_____
_____
_____
_____
_____
_____
_____
_____
_____
_____
_____
_____
_____
_____
_____
_____
_____

"Nothing can happen until you have started...Now is the time to get your course charted..." Glenn Rudin

* * * * * * * * * * * * * * * * * *

A BRAND IN YOUR HAND

Use this journal to take notes, record your thoughts and develop important details.

Today is: / / I am working on my:

Non-Verbal Brand   **Message**   **Colors**   **Elevator Pitch**   **Features**

Personal Brand   **Audience**   **Logo**   **Mission Statement**   **Benefits**

_____

_____

_____

_____

_____

_____

_____

_____

_____

_____

_____

_____

_____

_____

_____

_____

_____

_____

_____

_____

_____

_____

_____

_____

_____

"Nothing can happen until you have started...Now is the time to get your course charted..." Glenn Rudin

www.ABRANDINYOURHAND.com

A BRAND IN YOUR HAND

Use this journal to take notes, record your thoughts and develop important details.

Today is: / / I am working on my:

| Non-Verbal Brand | Message | Colors | Elevator Pitch | Features |
| Personal Brand | Audience | Logo | Mission Statement | Benefits |

_____
_____
_____
_____
_____
_____
_____
_____
_____
_____
_____
_____
_____
_____
_____
_____
_____
_____
_____
_____
_____
_____
_____
_____
_____
_____
_____
_____
_____
_____

"Nothing can happen until you have started...Now is the time to get your course charted..." Glenn Rudin

✶ ✶ ✶ ✶ ✶ ✶ ✶ ✶ ✶ ✶ ✶ ✶ ✶ ✶ ✶ ✶

A BRAND IN YOUR HAND

Use this journal to take notes, record your thoughts and develop important details.

Today is: / / I am working on my:

| Non-Verbal Brand | Message | Colors | Elevator Pitch | Features |
| Personal Brand | Audience | Logo | Mission Statement | Benefits |

_____
_____
_____
_____
_____
_____
_____
_____
_____
_____
_____
_____
_____
_____
_____
_____
_____
_____
_____
_____
_____
_____
_____
_____
_____
_____
_____
_____
_____
_____

"Nothing can happen until you have started...Now is the time to get your course charted..." Glenn Rudin

* * * * * * * * * * * * * * * * * * *

A BRAND IN YOUR HAND

Use this journal to take notes, record your thoughts and develop important details.

Today is: / / I am working on my:

Non-Verbal Brand	**Message**	**Colors**	**Elevator Pitch**	**Features**
Personal Brand	**Audience**	**Logo**	**Mission Statement**	**Benefits**

_____
_____
_____
_____
_____
_____
_____
_____
_____
_____
_____
_____
_____
_____
_____
_____
_____
_____
_____
_____
_____
_____
_____
_____
_____
_____
_____

"Nothing can happen until you have started...Now is the time to get your course charted..." Glenn Rudin

* * * * * * * * * * * * * * * * * *

A BRAND IN YOUR HAND

Use this journal to take notes, record your thoughts and develop important details.

Today is: / / I am working on my:

| Non-Verbal Brand | Message | Colors | Elevator Pitch | Features |
| Personal Brand | Audience | Logo | Mission Statement | Benefits |

_____

_____

_____

_____

_____

_____

_____

_____

_____

_____

_____

_____

_____

_____

_____

_____

_____

_____

_____

_____

_____

_____

_____

_____

_____

_____

_____

_____

_____

_____

_____

"Nothing can happen until you have started...Now is the time to get your course charted..." Glenn Rudin

A BRAND IN YOUR HAND

Use this journal to take notes, record your thoughts and develop important details.

Today is: / / *I am working on my:*

Non-Verbal Brand	**Message**	**Colors**	**Elevator Pitch**	**Features**
Personal Brand	**Audience**	**Logo**	**Mission Statement**	**Benefits**

_____
_____
_____
_____
_____
_____
_____
_____
_____
_____
_____
_____
_____
_____
_____
_____
_____
_____
_____
_____
_____
_____
_____
_____
_____
_____
_____

"Nothing can happen until you have started...Now is the time to get your course charted..." Glenn Rudin

✴ ✴ ✴ ✴ ✴ ✴ ✴ ✴ ✴ ✴ ✴ ✴ ✴ ✴ ✴ ✴

A BRAND IN YOUR HAND

Use this journal to take notes, record your thoughts and develop important details.

Today is: / / I am working on my:

Non-Verbal Brand	**Message**	**Colors**	**Elevator Pitch**	**Features**
Personal Brand	**Audience**	**Logo**	**Mission Statement**	**Benefits**

_____

_____

_____

_____

_____

_____

_____

_____

_____

_____

_____

_____

_____

_____

_____

_____

_____

_____

_____

_____

_____

_____

_____

_____

_____

"Nothing can happen until you have started...Now is the time to get your course charted..." Glenn Rudin

A BRAND IN YOUR HAND

Use this journal to take notes, record your thoughts and develop important details.

Today is: / /   I am working on my:

| Non-Verbal Brand | Message | Colors | Elevator Pitch | Features |
| Personal Brand | Audience | Logo | Mission Statement | Benefits |

_____

_____

_____

_____

_____

_____

_____

_____

_____

_____

_____

_____

_____

_____

_____

_____

_____

_____

_____

_____

_____

_____

_____

_____

_____

_____

_____

_____

"Nothing can happen until you have started...Now is the time to get your course charted..." Glenn Rudin

A BRAND IN YOUR HAND

Use this journal to take notes, record your thoughts and develop important details.

Today is: /   /   I am working on my:

Non-Verbal Brand	**Message**	**Colors**	**Elevator Pitch**	**Features**
Personal Brand	**Audience**	**Logo**	**Mission Statement**	**Benefits**

_____
_____
_____
_____
_____
_____
_____
_____
_____
_____
_____
_____
_____
_____
_____
_____
_____
_____
_____
_____
_____
_____
_____
_____
_____

"Nothing can happen until you have started...Now is the time to get your course charted..." Glenn Rudin

www.ABRANDINYOURHAND.com

A BRAND IN YOUR HAND

Use this journal to take notes, record your thoughts and develop important details.

Today is: / / I am working on my:

| Non-Verbal Brand | Message | Colors | Elevator Pitch | Features |
| Personal Brand | Audience | Logo | Mission Statement | Benefits |

_____
_____
_____
_____
_____
_____
_____
_____
_____
_____
_____
_____
_____
_____
_____
_____
_____
_____
_____
_____
_____
_____
_____
_____
_____
_____
_____
_____

"Nothing can happen until you have started...Now is the time to get your course charted..." Glenn Rudin

✱ ✱ ✱ ✱ ✱ ✱ ✱ ✱ ✱ ✱ ✱ ✱ ✱ ✱ ✱ ✱ ✱ ✱

A BRAND IN YOUR HAND

Use this journal to take notes, record your thoughts and develop important details.

Today is: / / I am working on my:

Non-Verbal Brand	**Message**	**Colors**	**Elevator Pitch**	**Features**
Personal Brand	**Audience**	**Logo**	**Mission Statement**	**Benefits**

_____

_____

_____

_____

_____

_____

_____

_____

_____

_____

_____

_____

_____

_____

_____

_____

_____

_____

_____

_____

_____

_____

_____

_____

_____

_____

"Nothing can happen until you have started...Now is the time to get your course charted..." Glenn Rudin

A BRAND IN YOUR HAND

Use this journal to take notes, record your thoughts and develop important details.

Today is: / / I am working on my:

| Non-Verbal Brand | Message | Colors | Elevator Pitch | Features |
| Personal Brand | Audience | Logo | Mission Statement | Benefits |

_____
_____
_____
_____
_____
_____
_____
_____
_____
_____
_____
_____
_____
_____
_____
_____
_____
_____
_____
_____
_____
_____
_____
_____
_____
_____
_____

"Nothing can happen until you have started...Now is the time to get your course charted..." Glenn Rudin

✶ ✶ ✶ ✶ ✶ ✶ ✶ ✶ ✶ ✶ ✶ ✶ ✶ ✶ ✶ ✶ ✶

A BRAND IN YOUR HAND

Use this journal to take notes, record your thoughts and develop important details.

Today is: / / *I am working on my:*

| Non-Verbal Brand | Message | Colors | Elevator Pitch | Features |
| Personal Brand | Audience | Logo | Mission Statement | Benefits |

_____

_____

_____

_____

_____

_____

_____

_____

_____

_____

_____

_____

_____

_____

_____

_____

_____

_____

_____

_____

_____

_____

_____

_____

_____

_____

_____

_____

"Nothing can happen until you have started...Now is the time to get your course charted..." Glenn Rudin

A BRAND IN YOUR HAND

✱ ✱ ✱ ✱ ✱ ✱ ✱ ✱ ✱ ✱ ✱ ✱ ✱ ✱ ✱ ✱ ✱ ✱

Use this journal to take notes, record your thoughts and develop important details.

Today is: / / I am working on my:

| Non-Verbal Brand | Message | Colors | Elevator Pitch | Features |
| Personal Brand | Audience | Logo | Mission Statement | Benefits |

_____
_____
_____
_____
_____
_____
_____
_____
_____
_____
_____
_____
_____
_____
_____
_____
_____
_____
_____
_____
_____
_____
_____
_____
_____
_____

"Nothing can happen until you have started...Now is the time to get your course charted..." Glenn Rudin

A **BRAND** in **YOUR HAND**

✱ ✱ ✱ ✱ ✱ ✱ ✱ ✱ ✱ ✱ ✱ ✱ ✱ ✱ ✱ ✱ ✱ ✱

Use this journal to take notes, record your thoughts and develop important details.

Today is: / / I am working on my:

Non-Verbal Brand	**Message**	**Colors**	**Elevator Pitch**	**Features**
Personal Brand	**Audience**	**Logo**	**Mission Statement**	**Benefits**

_____
_____
_____
_____
_____
_____
_____
_____
_____
_____
_____
_____
_____
_____
_____
_____
_____
_____
_____
_____
_____
_____
_____
_____
_____
_____
_____
_____
_____

"Nothing can happen until you have started...Now is the time to get your course charted..." Glenn Rudin

A BRAND IN YOUR HAND

✶ ✶ ✶ ✶ ✶ ✶ ✶ ✶ ✶ ✶ ✶ ✶ ✶ ✶ ✶ ✶ ✶ ✶

Use this journal to take notes, record your thoughts and develop important details.

Today is: / / I am working on my:

| Non-Verbal Brand | Message | Colors | Elevator Pitch | Features |
| Personal Brand | Audience | Logo | Mission Statement | Benefits |

_____
_____
_____
_____
_____
_____
_____
_____
_____
_____
_____
_____
_____
_____
_____
_____
_____
_____
_____
_____
_____
_____
_____
_____
_____
_____
_____

"Nothing can happen until you have started...Now is the time to get your course charted..." Glenn Rudin

* * * * * * * * * * * * * * * * * * *

A BRAND IN YOUR HAND

Use this journal to take notes, record your thoughts and develop important details.

Today is: / / I am working on my:

Non-Verbal Brand	**Message**	**Colors**	**Elevator Pitch**	**Features**
Personal Brand	**Audience**	**Logo**	**Mission Statement**	**Benefits**

_____
_____
_____
_____
_____
_____
_____
_____
_____
_____
_____
_____
_____
_____
_____
_____
_____
_____
_____
_____
_____
_____
_____
_____
_____
_____
_____

"Nothing can happen until you have started...Now is the time to get your course charted..." Glenn Rudin

A BRAND in YOUR HAND

Use this journal to take notes, record your thoughts and develop important details.

Today is: / / *I am working on my:*

| Non-Verbal Brand | Message | Colors | Elevator Pitch | Features |
| Personal Brand | Audience | Logo | Mission Statement | Benefits |

_____
_____
_____
_____
_____
_____
_____
_____
_____
_____
_____
_____
_____
_____
_____
_____
_____
_____
_____
_____
_____
_____
_____
_____
_____
_____
_____

"Nothing can happen until you have started...Now is the time to get your course charted..." Glenn Rudin

* * * * * * * * * * * * * * * * *

A BRAND IN YOUR HAND

Use this journal to take notes, record your thoughts and develop important details.

Today is: / / I am working on my:

Non-Verbal Brand	**Message**	**Colors**	**Elevator Pitch**	**Features**
Personal Brand	**Audience**	**Logo**	**Mission Statement**	**Benefits**

_____
_____
_____
_____
_____
_____
_____
_____
_____
_____
_____
_____
_____
_____
_____
_____
_____
_____
_____
_____
_____
_____
_____
_____
_____
_____
_____
_____
_____

"Nothing can happen until you have started...Now is the time to get your course charted..." Glenn Rudin

A BRAND IN YOUR HAND

Use this journal to take notes, record your thoughts and develop important details.

Today is: / / I am working on my:

Non-Verbal Brand	**Message**	**Colors**	**Elevator Pitch**	**Features**
Personal Brand	**Audience**	**Logo**	**Mission Statement**	**Benefits**

_____
_____
_____
_____
_____
_____
_____
_____
_____
_____
_____
_____
_____
_____
_____
_____
_____
_____
_____
_____
_____
_____
_____
_____
_____
_____
_____
_____
_____
_____

"Nothing can happen until you have started...Now is the time to get your course charted..." Glenn Rudin

✶ ✶ ✶ ✶ ✶ ✶ ✶ ✶ ✶ ✶ ✶ ✶ ✶ ✶ ✶ ✶ ✶ ✶

A BRAND IN YOUR HAND

Use this journal to take notes, record your thoughts and develop important details.

Today is: / / I am working on my:

Non-Verbal Brand	**Message**	**Colors**	**Elevator Pitch**	**Features**
Personal Brand	**Audience**	**Logo**	**Mission Statement**	**Benefits**

_____

_____

_____

_____

_____

_____

_____

_____

_____

_____

_____

_____

_____

_____

_____

_____

_____

_____

_____

_____

_____

_____

_____

_____

_____

_____

_____

"Nothing can happen until you have started...Now is the time to get your course charted..." Glenn Rudin

A BRAND IN YOUR HAND

Use this journal to take notes, record your thoughts and develop important details.

Today is: / / *I am working on my:*

| **Non-Verbal Brand** | **Message** | **Colors** | **Elevator Pitch** | **Features** |
| **Personal Brand** | **Audience** | **Logo** | **Mission Statement** | **Benefits** |

_____

_____

_____

_____

_____

_____

_____

_____

_____

_____

_____

_____

_____

_____

_____

_____

_____

_____

_____

_____

_____

_____

_____

_____

_____

_____

_____

_____

_____

_____

"Nothing can happen until you have started...Now is the time to get your course charted..." Glenn Rudin

www.ABRANDINYOURHAND.com

A BRAND in YOUR HAND

Use this journal to take notes, record your thoughts and develop important details.

Today is: / / I am working on my:

Non-Verbal Brand	Message	Colors	Elevator Pitch	Features
Personal Brand	Audience	Logo	Mission Statement	Benefits

_____

_____

_____

_____

_____

_____

_____

_____

_____

_____

_____

_____

_____

_____

_____

_____

_____

_____

_____

_____

_____

_____

_____

_____

_____

_____

_____

_____

_____

"Nothing can happen until you have started...Now is the time to get your course charted..." Glenn Rudin

www.ABRANDINYOURHAND.com

A BRAND IN YOUR HAND

Use this journal to take notes, record your thoughts and develop important details.

Today is: / /   I am working on my:

Non-Verbal Brand	**Message**	**Colors**	**Elevator Pitch**	**Features**
Personal Brand	**Audience**	**Logo**	**Mission Statement**	**Benefits**

_____
_____
_____
_____
_____
_____
_____
_____
_____
_____
_____
_____
_____
_____
_____
_____
_____
_____
_____
_____
_____
_____
_____
_____
_____
_____
_____

"Nothing can happen until you have started...Now is the time to get your course charted..." Glenn Rudin

A **BRAND** IN **YOUR HAND**

✴ ✴ ✴ ✴ ✴ ✴ ✴ ✴ ✴ ✴ ✴ ✴ ✴ ✴ ✴ ✴ ✴ ✴ ✴

Use this journal to take notes, record your thoughts and develop important details.

Today is: / / I am working on my:

| **Non-Verbal Brand** | **Message** | **Colors** | **Elevator Pitch** | **Features** |
| **Personal Brand** | **Audience** | **Logo** | **Mission Statement** | **Benefits** |

_____

_____

_____

_____

_____

_____

_____

_____

_____

_____

_____

_____

_____

_____

_____

_____

_____

_____

_____

_____

_____

_____

_____

_____

_____

_____

"Nothing can happen until you have started...Now is the time to get your course charted..." Glenn Rudin

www.ABRANDINYOURHAND.com

Acknowledgements

I'd like to acknowledge the following people who have made a difference in my life or have been instrumental in the creation of this book.

Dad——It's been over 40 years since you died so suddenly, but you will never be forgotten. The lessons I learned from you will never leave me nor will my memories of the great father you were.

Mom—You always fed my creative spirit. Thanks for taking an interest in my poems and photos and teaching me the importance of making personal contacts as well as having a sense of humor.
My greatest sadness is that neither of you will see this work.

Lisa—Thank you for being by my side and pushing me to be better and to keep striving for excellence. Your insight into the editing of this book is greatly appreciated.

Joshua and **Scott**—My love of reading Dr. Seuss books to you so long ago has never left me and was a catalyst for this book. See my About The Author page.

Coby—Thank you for your support and for always having the tech answers when I need them.

Wendy—I am lucky to have a big sister like you. Your love of my creative endeavors always spurs me to want to create more and more.

Rickee—I am also lucky to have a big sister like you. Thanks for all you've taught me over the years.

Mark—Thanks for your support and friendship since childhood.

To my book colleagues:

Martha Bullen—Your professionalism, positive spirit and appreciation of my work and direction in moving me from my concept and early verses to execution has been invaluable.

Niki Giokas—I appreciate your talent and your beautiful execution of my visions for the illustrations in the book.

Christy Collins—Thank you for turning the words and illustrations into a reality with your special touch.

David Aretha—I can't thank you enough for looking over my manuscript and adding your editing smarts.

I would love to hear about your new brand
Did I provide you with a helping hand?
By now you've become a branding phenom
Let me know at ABrandInYourHand.com.

Glenn@ABrandInYourHand.com
www.ABrandInYourHand.com

About Glenn Rudin and
A Brand In Your Hand

Sometimes we do things because "that's what we are supposed to do." We pick a college, we pick a major, we graduate, we pick a profession, we find a job, and hopefully we make a living. How many of us do this according to a plan? Conversely, how many of us just drift along with the current in the ocean of life? We bob along in the waves until one day we wash ashore somewhere and begin to make the best of it. I think far too many of us fall into the latter scenario.

I have had a long career in sales, product development and marketing and enjoy expressing my creativity, which is why I named by company Always Been Creative. I'm a branding expert and help people and businesses find their message. I wanted my first book to be much more creative than just offering tips on branding and messaging.

I've always been entertained and inspired by Theodor Geisel (the great Dr. Seuss). What child could resist the smart aleck Cat in the Hat? Who couldn't relate to Horton? The first book I can recall featured Bartholomew and the Oobleck. Imagine a world full of Oobleck...

When Dr. Seuss released *Oh, the Places You'll Go!* in 1990, I was transported to a wonderful place where anything was possible. I read this book to my young sons over and over, and I would slip their names into a particular passage and see their eyes light up with the possibilities this created for them.

Thirty years later I can still remember reading my young sons off to sleep.

So meaningful was this memory for me that when both of my sons graduated from law school, I gave them each a copy of *Oh, the Places You'll Go!* And of course, I penciled in their names to the same passage just like I did when they were kids.

Only recently, as I began to think about writing my own book, I began to wonder...What happens after you get to the places you'll go?

What if I could help readers continue this journey and figure out what to do before they've arrived at their places in life? What if I could help them not just drift along and learn to navigate the landing spot they saw for themselves?

That is why I decided to create a serious rhyming book for adults. However, my book does take a serious look at key topics like personal branding, creating an elevator pitch, business branding, and more. I've even created worksheets and journal pages to help you apply these lessons to your own life and business.

My goal in writing this book is to help you create the authentic brand of yourself so you can chart your course and come ashore precisely where you want to be.

Armed with this knowledge and knowhow, you will have a much better sense of who you are, what you stand for and where you are going. After all, if you are aware of these things, then you can be in control. And, when you know who you are from a branding sense, it makes it much easier for us to know about this as well.

I hope this book helps you have a more pleasant journey through your ocean of life. I wish you sincere good luck finding the brand you have in your hand.